DIONYSOS AND THE PIRATES

AND THE PIRATES

Homeric Hymn Number Seven

Translated by PENELOPE PRODDOW
Illustrated by BARBARA COONEY

Doubleday & Company, Inc., Garden City, New York

Library of Congress Catalog Card Number: 76-91410.
Copyright © 1970 by Doubleday & Company, Inc. All Rights Reserved.
Printed in the United States of America.

9 8 7 6 5 4 3 2

ISBN: 0-385-01343-4 TRADE
      0-385-03193-9 PREBOUND

For John R. Webster

I will tell of Dionysos,
the son of beautiful Semele,
how he appeared on the cliffs
by the shore of the unharvested, salt sea,
like a youth,
fresh in the bloom of manhood.

His shining, black hair fell in abundance,
and over his powerful shoulders
he wore a purple cloak.

But men from a ship with gliding oars,
Tyrsenian pirates,
were stealing
over the wine-dark water.

(A terrible fate led them on.)

Spotting the youth, they nodded
one to another,
and without delay, sprang ashore.

Capturing him quickly,
they brought him aboard their ship,
rejoicing.

They thought him the son
of Zeus-favored kings,
and they tried to bind him
with cutting fetters.

Yet the knots would not hold
and the fetters dropped away
from his hands and feet.

And Dionysos sat idly,
smiling with dark blue eyes.

Watching him, the helmsman
cried aloud in haste:

"Madmen!" he addressed his comrades.
"What god is this you have seized
  and now would bind?
  Do you not see his strength?
  Our well-built ship cannot carry him.

"Surely he is Zeus,
  Apollo of the silver bow, or possibly
  Poseidon.
  For he does not look like mortal men,
  but the gods who live on Olympus.

"Come. Let us set him free on the darkening coast.
  At once!
  Don't touch him,
  lest he, enraged, hurl forth against us
  biting winds and violent tempests."

He spoke,
but the captain mocked him,
scornfully.

"Madman yourself!" he cried.
"See the fair breeze.
Now pull on the ropes
and hoist the sail of the ship.
The youth is our charge, not yours.

"He was bound, I wager, for Egypt,
Cyprus, the Hyperboreans,
or lands beyond.

"But, in the end, he'll reveal
his friends,
his great wealth,
and the names of his brothers, — since
fate has thrown him to us."

Still scoffing,
he had the mast and sail raised aloft
on the ship.

Then wind breathed into the heart of the sail
and the crew pulled the ropes tight
on either side.

Suddenly,
strange things were seen
about them.

First, throughout the swift, dark ship
wine flowed,
sweet-smelling and delicious,
and there arose
the fragrance of ambrosia.

Amazement seized the gaping crew.

All at once, a vine spread
in both directions
across the top of the sail,
and endless clusters of grapes
were swinging from it.

Dark ivy spiraled up the mast
in circles,
bursting with blossoms,
and rich berries
were sprouting upon it.

And all the pins
which held the oars
were wreathed
in flowery garlands.

The sailors, watching it,
shouted at the helmsman finally
to steer their ship to land.

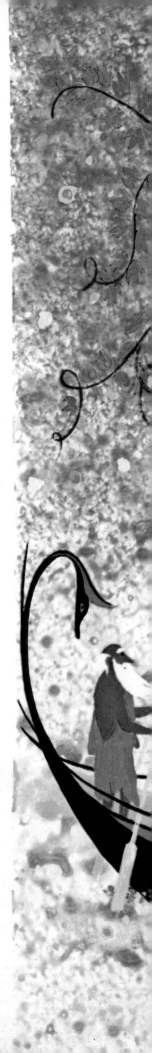

But the youth in the bow of the vessel
turned himself
into a majestic lion that growled
loudly.

In the middle of the ship,
he showed his power
with another sign.

He created a bear with a shaggy neck.

It reared up, hungrily, —

while on the higher deck
the lion remained,
untamed, and glaring savagely.

The sailors fled to the stern.

They huddled in terror
around the wise helmsman.

The lion, hurtling speedily towards them,
pounced upon their captain.

And, when they saw it, the rest of the crew
leapt overboard together
into the shimmering sea
to escape a terrible fate.

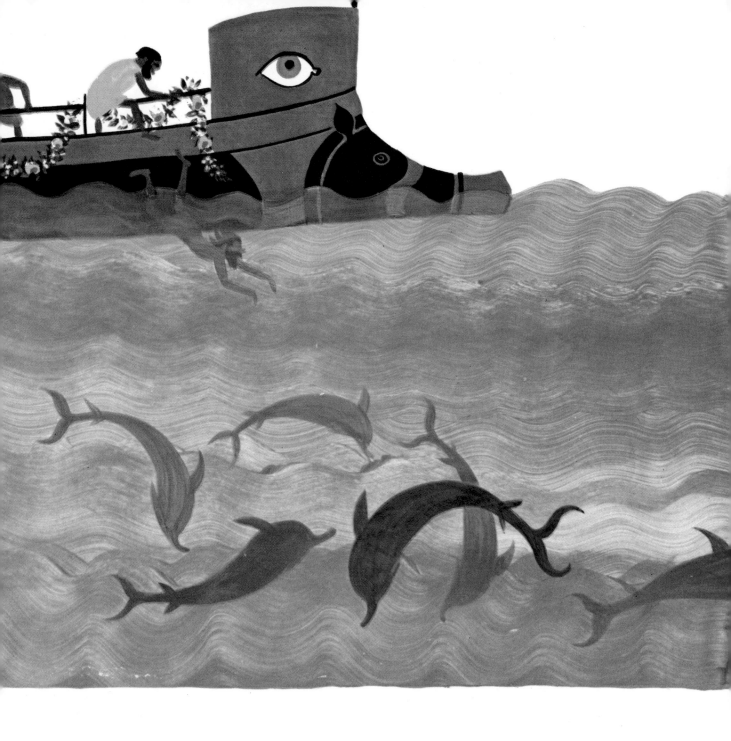

And they were turned to
dolphins.

But Dionysos, pitying the helmsman,
held him back,
and cheered him with these words:

"Rejoice!" he said.
"You have pleased my heart.
 For I am joyous Dionysos, the god
 whom Semele, my mother, the daughter of Cadmus,
 bore to Zeus in love."

Hail to you, Dionysos, son of fair Semele.

He who forgets you
can never fashion sweet song.

TRANSLATOR'S NOTE

Dionysos and the Pirates is the seventh in a collection of hymns , known as the Homeric Hymns, which were used by Greek min-strels as introductions to their longer songs.

Such a hymn would invoke the god in whose honor a feast was being given, praising his lineage and his achievements. It was hoped that the god would then feel kindly towards the minstrel and favor all the songs that followed.

The hymn itself is a very ancient form and appears in vari-ous localities of Greece at different times. Dionysos and the Pirates could have been written as early as the seventh century B.C. or as late as the third.

CAST OF CHARACTERS AND PLACES

Apollo   He was the god of music, but along with his lyre he carried a bow with deadly arrows.

Cadmus   He was the founder of Thebes, and because he had married Harmonia, the daughter of the goddess of love, he was a king much favored by Zeus.

Dionysos   He was one of the foremost Greek gods—the god of all growing things, especially the grapevine and the ivy, and assorted animals. He was also the god of the theater.

The Hyperboreans A people who lived in perfect happiness in a land that lay behind the north wind.

Poseidon   He was the moody and violent god of the sea.

Semele   This golden-haired princess of Thebes, the youngest daughter of King Cadmus, was the mother of Dionysos.

Tyrsenian Pirates They were barbarians from the north of Greece.

Zeus   He was the king of the gods and Dionysos' father. One of his attributes was the thunderbolt, which he wielded frequently.

Penelope Proddow was graduated from Miss Porter's School and Bryn Mawr College where she received her degree in Classical and Near Eastern Archeology. She is an alumna of the American School of Classical Studies at Athens and divides her time between Greenwich, Connecticut, and Greece.

Caldecott medal winner **Barbara Cooney** has illustrated more than seventy children's books. She was born in Brooklyn, New York, majored in art at Smith College and also studied at the Art Students League. Miss Cooney went on a special trip to Greece to do on-the-spot research for this book, before going on to visit her married daughter, Gretel, in India. She lives in Pepperell, Massachusetts, with her husband, Dr. Charles Talbot Porter. They have four children, Gretel, Barnaby, Charles Jr., and Phoebe.